Additional Core Reading from:

Claire Capon, *Understanding Organisational Context*, Second Edition

We work with leading authors to develop the strongest educational materials bringing cutting-edge thinking and best learning practice to a global market.

Under a range of well-known imprints, including Financial Times/Prentice Hall, Addison Wesley and Longman, we craft high quality print and electronic publications which help readers to understand and apply their content, whether studying or at work.

Pearson Custom Publishing enables our customers to access a wide and expanding range of market-leading content from world-renowned authors and develop their own tailor-made book. You choose the content that meets your needs and Pearson Custom Publishing produces a high-quality printed book.

To find out more about custom publishing, visit www.pearsoncustom.co.uk

A Pearson Custom Publication

Additional Core Reading from:
Claire Capon, *Understanding Organisational Context,*
Second Edition

Compiled from:

Understanding Organisational Context:
Inside and Outside Organisations
Second Edition
by Claire Capon

PEARSON
Custom
Publishing

Pearson Education Limited
Edinburgh Gate
Harlow
Essex CM20 2JE

And associated companies throughout the world

Visit us on the World Wide Web at:
www.pearsoned.co.uk

First published 2010

This Custom Book Edition © 2010 Published by Pearson Education Limited

Compiled from:

Understanding Organisational Context: Inside and Outside Organisations
Second Edition
by Claire Capon
ISBN 978 0 273 67660 7
Copyright © Pearson Education Limited 2000, 2004

ISBN 978 1 84959 230 7

Printed and bound in Great Britain by Henry Ling Limited at the Dorset Press,
Dorchester, DT1 1HD

Contents

The following content is from:

Understanding Organisational Context:
Inside and Outside Organisations
Second Edition
by Claire Capon

SWOT Analysis

SWOT analysis and the organisation

SWOT stands for strengths, weaknesses, opportunities and threats, and analysis of these gives an overview of the position an organisation finds itself in, vis à via its external environment. The strengths and weaknesses of an organisation arise from its internal environment, namely resourses and their use, structure, culture and the tasks carried out by the four functions of business (marketing, operations management, finance and HRM) – refer to Chapters 4, 5, 6 and 7 respectively. Which strengths an organisation decides to build on and which weaknesses it seeks to minimise depends on the impact of opportunities and threats from the external environment. The identification of external influences on an organisation is aided by the use of PEST analysis, LoNGPEST analysis, competitor analysis and market analysis – refer to Chapters 8, 9, 10 and 4 respectively. Once the external influences on an organisation have been identified, they can then be judged to be either a threat or opportunity and be dealt with or taken advantage of as appropriate.

Strengths

A strength is a competence, valuable resource or attribute that an organisation uses to exploit opportunities in the external environment or to help it counter threats from the external environment. Strengths could include a resource such as a well-motivated and skilled workforce, with low turnover, or an attribute such as a strongly established brand image or reputation. Examples include Cadbury's Dairy Milk brand and Marks and Spencer's reputation for good quality.

Stakeholders and key success factors

Customers are stakeholders in an organisation and fulfilling key success factors involves the organisation in meeting the needs and expectations of its customers and other stakeholders (*see* earlier in this chapter). For example, a key success factor may be a good relationship with a reliable supplier. This will be especially true if the supplier is the only supplier or one of very few supplying a key component or part. Meeting the key success factors will require the organisation to meet the supplier's expectations, which will include regular orders of a certain minimum size, with little room for negotiation on price if the supplier is powerful.

In seeking to satisfy stakeholders, especially customers, while at the same time outperforming competitors, organisations should seek to:

- fulfil the key success factors for the industry or market;
- develop competencies that provide competitive advantage (*see* discussion on competitive advantage and premium prices);
- utilise competencies to meet the requirements of specific customers and aim to charge a premium price.

Competitive advantage and premium prices

Competitive advantage arises from the unique features or 'extras' that a product or service possesses and for which customers are prepared to pay a higher or premium price. For example, some dry cleaners offer a standard service and a gold service. The standard service includes dry cleaning the item of clothing, pressing it by machine and returning the item to its owner on a cheap hanger with a polythene cover over it. In contrast, the gold service includes dry cleaning the garment, hand pressing and finishing it before it is returned to its owner on a more robust hanger and in a more substantial plastic cover. There will be a small group of customers who will be prepared to pay a higher or premium price for the extras that the gold service provides. Being able to offer the gold service will give the dry cleaner a competitive advantage over nearby dry cleaners who do not offer this service.

Weaknesses

A weakness is defined as lacking a competence, resource or attribute that an organisation needs to perform better than its competitors in the external environment. A company producing tableware for the domestic and catering markets will rely in part on styling and designs to make products appealing to customers. If it relies on the designs that have always been used or occasionally on shopfloor staff coming up with new patterns, it is likely to lack competence in design, a key success factor for the tableware industry. The lack of a key resource, such as a new piece of technologically advanced equipment, is also a weakness, particularly if your competitors have access to that equipment.

Opportunities

Opportunities are openings or chances in the external environment or marketplace that an organisation may pursue to obtain benefits. The identification of a new geographic market in North America for a firm's products is an opportunity. Such opportunities can be exploited by manufacturing the product in the firm's home country and exporting it to North America, or by forming a strategic alliance with a local US company and having the benefits of the greater understanding of the local and national external environment offered by that partner in the strategic alliance. This type of arrangement will also need to confer benefits on the alliance partner, otherwise it is unlikely to be successful in the long term. The third alternative is to manufacture the product locally, which is perhaps the most time and resource consuming of the three options as it involves setting up from scratch in a foreign country. This will be more difficult than operating in a home environment or with advice from an organisation for which the foreign market is a home environment.

Key success factors

The degree to which an organisation is successful depends on its ability to meet its key success factors (KSF). Key success factors are what an organisation must do well and better than its competitors if it is to succeed. They can arise from a number of sources.

First, key success factors may be established by the industry in which an organisation operates. For example, in the clothes mail-order business, being able to provide speedy delivery to the customer's home is a key success factor for all companies in the industry. Second, key success factors may be determined by the organisation itself. When the Midland Bank set up telephone banking with its subsidiary First Direct, the key success factors were to provide an accurate banking service that required a minimum amount of paperwork, could be accessed 24 hours a day, and did away with the need for high-street branches. Other banks have adopted these key success factors by providing their own telephone banking services and will continue to try to meet these key success factors by providing banking services in the home via the internet.

Finally, key success factors may be signified by customers indicating that they require products with particular features or services. One example is the demand from consumers for high-quality take-away coffee from coffee bars and sandwich shops. The demand from consumers is not only for high-quality coffee but also for a range of different types of coffee, from the familiar cappuccino and espresso to the more exotic sounding café latte, mocha and arabica. Therefore a key success factor for coffee and sandwich bars is the provision of a wider range of high-quality coffees.

Threats

Threats have the potential to damage an organisation's performance in the marketplace or external environment. Threats often arise from competitors or factors that are outside the control of the organisation. The competitor that cuts prices by 50 per cent today and the competitor that brings out a new generation of technologically advanced products both pose a clear threat to all other organisations operating in the same industry. Threats may also arise from changes in legislation or taxation relating to the industry in which an organisation operates. For example, the imposition of value added tax (VAT) on newspapers and books or children's clothes would affect both the manufacturers of such products and the amount of business done by retailers selling such products to members of the public.

Clearly, threats from the external environment may endanger an organisation. However, threats may also jeopardise good opportunities of which the organisation expects to take advantage. In 1997 the US company WorldCom tendered £19 billion for MCI, another US company. This offer outbid BT's proposal of £11 billion for MCI by over 70 per cent. The WorldCom offer became a realised threat that snatched an opportunity from under BT's nose and left a gap in the latter's strategy to secure a global partner.

Different types of SWOT analysis

The most basic SWOT analysis will examine how threats and opportunities can be dealt with while allowing the organisation to utilise its strengths and weaknesses to meet its key success factors. Merely producing long lists of threats, opportunities, weaknesses and strengths indicates a lack of thought and seriousness as regards the organisation. Lists should be brief and specific, indicating the key and important issues. The threats, opportunities, weaknesses and strengths should be judged and assessed in relative terms. For example, there is little merit in expressing the view that a particular strength or opportunity is 'good'. Its worth should be expressed relative to how a competitor fares with the same strength or opportunity. Organisations need to aim to be better than competitors when it comes to possessing strengths and exploiting opportunities. The same holds true for weaknesses and threats: organisations need to seek to minimise the effect of these to a greater extent than their competitors.

A basic SWOT analysis should discuss, illustrate and debate the threats, opportunities, weaknesses and strengths identified and how the organisation may build on the strengths, exploit the opportunities and minimise the weaknesses and threats to a greater extent than its competitors. This will include an assessment of where the company is at the current time and where it wishes to be at some point in the future. The organisation needs to decide how far away that future is – it will vary from a few months to many years depending on the organisation, the nature of its business and its current situation.

Guidelines for carrying out SWOT analysis

1 Identify key strengths, weaknesses, opportunities and threats. Do not produce a long list.
2 Once the key strengths, weaknesses, opportunities and threats have been identified, clear discussion and debate concerning them is required. The appropriate discussion and debate may be generated by considering the questions outlined below.

Strengths

Decide whether the organisation has the appropriate strengths on which to build and exploit its opportunities. How can it best exploit its strengths in relation to the opportunities available to it? Which strengths should the organisation seek to develop for the future?

Weaknesses

Decide whether remedying weaknesses is more urgent than building on strengths to exploit opportunities. Does ignoring important weaknesses make the organisation vulnerable to threats which could result in its going out of business or being taken over? How can critical weaknesses be offset or converted into strengths?

Opportunities

Identify new markets and market segments that might be suitable given the organisation's existing strengths and competencies. Identify changes that are occurring to existing customers and within existing markets. Consider using strategies of market penetration and market development to take advantage of any opportunities arising from existing and changing markets – *see* Chapter 4. Identify changes that need to be made to products and services. Consider strategies of product development and diversification to take advantage of any opportunities arising from changes to existing products – *see* Chapter 4.

Threats

Do threats need managing more urgently than the opportunities pursued? Which threats need to be dealt with immediately and in the short term? Which threats are issues for the organisation to consider when undertaking longer-term planning? How can critical threats be offset or turned into new opportunities?

Interflora

By Claire Capon

Interflora was founded in 1923 and is an association of florists owned by its members, which today is the largest UK flower delivery organisation, supplying four million bouquets annually, worth over £60m. The florists who belong to Interflora accept orders from around the world for flowers to be delivered in their local neighbourhood. Membership of Interflora allows co-ordination of flower deliveries and the organisation provides computer terminals for participating shops and clearing payments between its members. The updating proposals discussed in this case study proposed an increase in a florist's annual subscription charge for belonging to Interflora from £300 to £1750 and a reduction in the cost of each transaction from £2.99 to 60p.

Interflora and its affairs are managed by the members via an elected board of directors. Doug McGrath was identified by headhunters and in January 1996 was appointed chief executive of Interflora. He was recruited to update and overhaul the association, which was viewed by the board as a cosy trade organisation with traditional values. This was considered uncommercial and uncompetitive by Doug McGrath and the Interflora board. The updating was to take the form of the introduction of a corporate and commercial attitude to conducting business.

The updating of Interflora was announced at the organisation's 1996 Bournemouth conference. It was revealed by Doug McGrath and David Parry that Interflora was to have a mission statement and modern management thinking was to be introduced to the organisation to solve the problems faced by the organisation and the membership. The reasoning centred around the fierce competition faced by florists from garages and supermarkets, some of which offered home delivery of bouquets, e.g. Marks & Spencer and Waitrose. The view taken by Doug McGrath and the commercially minded chairman, Bristol florist David Parry, was that Interflora should ditch its traditional family values and act like a modern corporation.

Potentially, McGrath and Parry could have been a strong team that could have been of considerable benefit to Interflora, with McGrath's considerable business experience and Parry's extensive knowledge and experience of the florist trade. The view expressed by Caroline Marshall-Foster, editor of the trade publication the *Florist*, was that floristry was potentially a very profitable business and it is probably the opportunity for profit that McGrath and Parry saw.

If Interflora were to behave like a modern corporation, Doug McGrath saw opportunities for the centralisation of activities such as the purchase of flowers, which would produce economies of scale and make Interflora the largest purchaser of flowers in the UK. This would mean that all the flowers bought by Interflora would be purchased collectively on behalf of the members, giving it the power to negotiate better deals with suppliers than if members brought their flowers individually. The policy of centralised purchasing would be introduced along with standardisation of many other facets of the service provided by Interflora florists, such as opening times, service and corporate image, e.g. window displays.

David Parry and Doug McGrath left the Bournemouth conference convinced that their presentation of an updated and modern Interflora had been successful and that the conference delegates supported the proposed changes. However, they had not read the mood of the conference correctly. In fact, Interflora members saw the presentation of Interflora's image standardisation as dictatorial. This was illustrated by the views and actions of Bev Woods, an Interflora member and florist.

Bev Woods ran a florist shop in Leeds and did not view the mission statement and proposals on standardisation as suitable for her shop, as Interflora work comprised only a small proportion of the total amount of work undertaken by her business. A policy document was issued to all Interflora members outlining and reinforcing the conference proposals. The general view of the membership was that the proposals would be expensive for small florists, who make up a significant proportion of Interflora's members, and hence posed a financial threat to the long-term survival of small florist shops.

Realising that the proposals had not been as well received as he had initially thought, Doug McGrath decided to hold face-to-face meetings with Interflora members who were unhappy with proposals presented at Bournemouth and in the policy document. At one of these meetings, Bev Woods challenged the board over a small administrative change that she thought could be illegal. This challenge was met with a patronising reply, and in response the other Interflora members present displayed considerable anger at the manner in which Bev Woods was treated.

Hence Bev Woods and a fellow florist from London, Rose-Marie Watkins, joined forces and sought to gain the 250 signatures necessary to call an extraordinary general meeting (EGM) of Interflora. This involved the two women in stuffing and addressing 2600 envelopes by hand. The letters were posted so that they would arrive on the doormats of Interflora members the day after Valentine's Day and three weeks before Mother's Day in 1997, making use of a slight lull in the business calendar of busy florists.

Having realised that the proposals presented at Bournemouth had not been well received, Doug McGrath dropped plans for the centralised purchasing of flowers and other proposals that 50 per cent or more of Interflora's members disagreed with or felt neutral about. This was in line with a poll of members conducted by Interflora management. The poll was a telephone survey of a sample of 611 out of 2600 members. The results showed that 65 per cent of members agreed with the proposed changes. This was not accepted by Bev Woods and Rose-Marie Watkins, who thought that the views of all 2600 members should be taken into account.

The efforts and timing of Bev Woods and Rose-Marie Watkins paid off and by Mother's Day 1997 enough signatures had been gathered to force an EGM to be held in May 1997. This interrupted the programme of change that Doug McGrath and David Parry wanted in place by 1 June 1997. Bev Woods and Rose-Marie Watkins appointed a solicitor to help them prepare for the EGM, which was viewed as crucial if Interflora members were to retain their rights under the memorandum and articles of association, which were to have disappeared under the planned changes. Assistance in the battle against the board was forthcoming in the shape of Geoff Hughes, an ambitious Bristol-based florist, viewed by many as a political animal with a strategic outlook.

Geoff Hughes' primary aim was to remove Doug McGrath, David Parry and the rest of the Interflora board, as they were viewed as the drivers of the proposed change. This went beyond Bev Woods' original intention, which was to see the structure of Interflora change, as she thought that it allowed board members too much power. Despite being over-ruled, Bev Woods remained very much an active figurehead in the campaign to oust the Interflora board. The aims pursued by Bev Woods, Rose-Marie Watkins and Geoff Hughes were to diminish board support and appoint a caretaker board, a proposal which sent shockwaves through the organisation.

Bev Woods and Rose-Marie Watkins were determined to win and prepared very carefully for the EGM, rehearsing their speeches and actions. At the EGM they, Geoff Hughes and other Interflora members all had board members to mark. The turnout at the EGM was substantial, with 1200 florists coming to Warwick University, three times the expected number. In the electric and gladiatorial atmosphere of the EGM, Bev Woods spoke

first and made an inspirational speech designed to get the support of non-committed Interflora members. The speech was even much admired by the opposition, Doug McGrath.

Rose-Marie Watkins employed cunning and laid a trap for David Parry to fall into. His role at the EGM was to chair the meeting and hence remain impartial. In her speech, Rose-Marie Watkins quoted from a recent *Daily Telegraph* article citing David Parry as stating that approximately 1000 Interflora members would cease to be members under the updating proposals. When this point was made, David Parry responded by rising to his feet to correct the remark by making a statement and in doing so breached his position as impartial chairman. This was raised as a point of order by Bev Woods, who indicated to him that by making a statement he was not being fair to both sides. The Interflora members present applauded. David Parry moved on to arguing with Geoff Hughes and the Interflora board continued to manage the meeting badly. A succession of Interflora members made speeches supporting the proposals of Bev Woods, Rose-Marie Watkins and Geoff Hughes.

There followed a much-needed lunch break. During lunch one Interflora member complained about the cold quiche buffet and in talking to the restaurant manager discovered that the amount paid for the lunch was £6 a head less than Interflora members had been charged. This was raised as a question in the afternoon session and it was suggested that the Interflora board was making money from its own members. This heightened the anger of the already hostile Interflora members and the meeting degenerated into an irate protest against the board. It was later clarified that the extra £6 a head was to cover the expenses of drinks, VAT and other extras.

The meeting was adjourned and voting took place, with board members waiting an anxious two hours for the results. These results removed all 13 board members, leaving Bev Woods, Rose-Marie Watkins and Geoff Hughes feeling ecstatic at their victory. However, a surprise was in store for the two women. The election of the new caretaker board saw their friend and ally Geoff Hughes moved into the role of chairman. It was from this position that he declared that he had never disagreed with business ideas of the previous board and he thought them appropriate.

In consequence, Geoff Hughes was not re-elected as chairman of Interflora in 1998. Interflora decided not to appoint a florist and Martin Redman, an accountant, was appointed chairman, not chief executive, of Interflora. There had been a radical change of personalities on the board of Interflora, but not of the aims that it was seeking to achieve.

Sources: Wolffe, R (1997) 'Interflora board ousted in protest over restructuring', *Financial Times*, 12 May 1998; 'Guns 'n' Posies', *Blood on the Carpet*, BBC2, 10 February 1999.

1 Identify the stakeholders in Interflora before the 1996 Bournemouth conference and plot them on a power and interest matrix.

2 Consider the situation that Interflora was in by the time of the EGM in May 1997. Identify any additions or deletions to the Interflora stakeholders you identified in answering question 1. Plot all the stakeholders you have identified in Interflora as they would appear in May 1997, immediately after the EGM at Warwick University.

3 What lessons are to be learned from the Interflora experience with regard to identifying and managing stakeholders?

For more case studies please visit www.booksites.net/capon

MANAGING CHANGE

The museum locked in the past

By Leslie Crawford

The Prado museum, Spain's top tourist attraction, has just under 12 months to get ready for the biggest expansion in its history, with the opening of three annexes that will double exhibition space for the world's finest collection of works by Goya, El Greco and Velazquez.

The expansion, which is long overdue, could turn out to be an unmitigated disaster. As things now stand, the Prado will have neither the budget nor the extra staff to run its bigger self. The looming crisis has triggered a heated debate about how Spain's leading museum should be managed and what degree of financial independence, if any, it should enjoy.

At the centre of the storm is Eduardo Serra, chairman of UBS Warburg in Spain and a former defence minister, who agreed to become the (unremunerated) chairman of the Prado's board of trustees 18 months ago. Mr Serra is candid about the museum's plight. The Prado, he says, 'is the great sick man of our culture'.

The catalogue of ills is as long as the Prado's history. In the early 19th century, the palace that houses the royal art collection was turned into a barracks by Napoleon's invading troops, who used statues and other works of art for target practice. More recently, a leaking roof forced the closure of the Velazquez rooms because rain was streaming down the walls.

Money is so tight that for several years the chief of security at the Prado has been 'on loan' from the police force. A government hiring freeze has also meant that the museum has not been allowed to fill 57 vacancies and must make do with only 350 staff – far fewer than at other European museums of similar size and importance.

Most frustrating of all is the fact that the Prado has no control over its finances. Its budget is set by the finance ministry and the museum must return any unspent money at the end of each year. The Prado is not allowed to operate a bank account and it cannot accept corporate sponsorship without the prior authorisation of Spain's finance ministry.

The museum last year turned down an offer of audio guides because the headsets bore the logo of a private telecommunications group. Only recently did it win special authorisation to publish a modest floor map for the 1.8m visitors it receives each year.

Few art-lovers would disagree with Mr Serra's diagnosis. The Prado, he says, is understaffed, underfunded and hamstrung by a legal framework that stifles all private initiative.

The remedy, however, is not straightforward. Mr Serra's plans for the modernisation of the Prado have clashed with the conservative views of Spain's art establishment. To them, Mr Serra is a merchant in their temple of high art; a philistine who would turn the Prado into a private playground for the rich.

Mr Serra's offence has been to argue that the Prado must be given more financial freedom and more control over its resources. He wants to treble the budget, to €45m (£28m), by 2005 and he wants to raise slightly more than half of this by the museum's own fundraising efforts.

Shrinking state subsidies mean that most museums in Europe have had to become active fundraisers. The Louvre in Paris now derives 40 per cent of its income from private sources, while the National Gallery in London meets a third of its running costs through donations, membership programmes and corporate sponsorship.

The Prado, however, has no such freedom. Mr Serra is campaigning for changes in the law, which limits private donations to the Prado to €300. As a result, the Foundation of the Friends of the Prado has only a few hundred members, who are offered no special privileges. 'I cannot send sponsors a magazine because we do not publish one,' Mr Serra laments. 'I cannot invite donors to special exhibitions because we stage so few of them.'

'Should we not make a greater effort to obtain private resources to make better use of public funds?' Mr Serra asked in a recent speech. 'This approach has been derided as a dangerous step towards the privatisation of the Prado. A dispassionate consideration of the problem would yield the very opposite conclusion.'

Few Spaniards, however, feel dispassionate about the Prado. As Mr Serra concedes: 'The Prado is the cultural symbol of Spain. To propose change is like laying your hands on the family silver. The very concept of modernising management is treated like a crime.'

At the heart of the debate is a tug-of-war between those who believe that the Prado's sole mission is to guard the national heritage and those, such as Mr Serra, who believe the museum should be more active in engaging the public, with a livelier educational programme and more frequent temporary exhibitions.

At present, a visit to the Prado is a dispiriting affair: there is little information for the layman, rooms are frequently closed to the public and there are only six guides for the thousands of tourists who arrive each day. The Prado knows little about its visitors: it keeps no records of their age or provenance, or how many of them have visited the museum before.

The expansion, however, will require radical changes to the way the museum is managed. The Boston Consulting Group, which is advising the Prado on its modernisation programme, estimates that staff numbers will have to double to 700 and that the museum will require 'a new management model that is much more geared towards attending the public'.

Mr Serra believes the museum's staff should be better paid. He would like to introduce a proper career structure, with annual performance reviews and promotion for those who do well.

Change, however, does not come easily to a crusty, 18th-century institution whose bureaucracy is as dark and as impenetrable as any of Goya's Black Paintings. The Prado's staff are civil servants with life-long tenure and, although they are pitifully paid, they are suspicious of Mr Serra's attempts to drag them into the 21st century. They are particularly wary of his plans to circumvent the government hiring freeze by getting special dispensation to employ non-civil service staff on temporary contracts. In a letter to the board of trustees last year, the Prado's

specialist staff rejected annual performance reviews and the carrot of better pay. They said they saw no reason for the Prado to change.

The clash between modernisers and traditionalists triggered the resignation last December of Fernando Checa, the Prado's director. Mr Checa, a mild-mannered art historian with a halo of fuzzy hair and large, tortoiseshell spectacles, accused Mr Serra of 'interfering too often in my relationship with the curators and with the museum's scientific staff'.

Mr Checa, a traditionalist, believed the scholarly integrity of the Prado was being undermined by Mr Serra's plans. His successor, Miguel Zugaza, who is credited with breathing new life into Bilbao's Museum of Fine Arts, is understood to be more in tune with the chairman's thinking.

Mr Zugaza and Mr Serra have only a few months to overcome the political, legal and bureaucratic obstacles that stand in the way of the Prado's modernisation. It will be a battle worthy of the great spectacles that are depicted in the halls of the museum, although it is to be hoped it will not be as bloody.

Source: Financial Times, 15 February 2002. Reprinted with permission.

Introduction

The first 11 chapters of this book have been concerned with understanding and analysing the tasks and activities which organisations undertake, along with the internal and external environments in which they operate. Hence this chapter examines how organisations cope with change from these environments and the tools and techniques that can aid organisations in planning for and managing change.

Sources of organisational change

The demand for change in organisations is caused by shifts in the external and internal environments in which they operate. External environmental factors were discussed in earlier chapters. The PEST issues – political, economic, sociocultural and technological – are drivers or sources of change that all organisations face. Additionally, the behaviour and demands of external stakeholders, including competitors, customers, financiers and shareholders, may drive change for an organisation. The influence an organisation has over these drivers of change is often limited, as they usually arise from another organisation or development over which the company has no or limited influence.

However, the actions of competitor companies or organisations which result in businesses having to change usually require a response. For example, the introduction of a price-cutting strategy by a competitor is clearly an event that requires an immediate reaction if a company is to retain market share.

The introduction of a new technology or technologically advanced product by a competitor will require a considered response that may take time to develop. Dyson's introduction of the bagless vacuum cleaner took the market by surprise and the company rapidly seized market share from other vacuum producers. Manufacturers of traditional vacuum cleaners took several years to develop a noticeable and competitive response to Dyson.

Internal sources or drivers of change include employees, trade unions and organisational departments. Demands from employees and trade unions for more pay and different wage and salary structures may mean that the rewards system operated by the organisation changes, although this is unlikely to happen in isolation. The likely outcome would be that a deal would be struck over working hours or productivity in return for improved wages and conditions of employment.

Therefore organisations have to assess the outcome of carrying on with current tasks and activities or decide to plan and implement change to allow the organisation to develop from its current position. The decision to implement change will depend on whether the organisation wants to maintain or increase market size. If an organisation is seeking to maintain market size, it should realise that this is a difficult task in declining markets and an easier task in stable or growing markets. Alternatively, if an organisation is aiming for market growth, it should recognise that this is most realistic if markets are growing, but still possible if markets are stable.

The decision to implement change requires an assessment of the resources available and those required. The difference between the two should be evaluated (*see* Chapter 1). Stakeholder behaviour, alongside current and changing expectations, should also be considered when planning for change (*see* Chapter 11). In the case of the Prado museum (see entry case study 12.1) it could be argued that the visitors, as stakeholders, expect enough guides, audio guides, maps, brochures and postcards, very little of which is currently provided by the Prado.

✓ Check your understanding

Do you understand the possible sources of change for organisations?

Check your understanding by identifying internal and external drivers of change and summarise how the drivers of change you have identified may impact on an organisation.

Types of organisational change

The changes that organisations choose to implement will cover many different aspects of organisational life. These changes can include alterations to organisational size, structure and culture, as well as changes to operational activities and the roles that people undertake in an organisation. Change is either reactive or proactive. Reactive change is where the organisation reacts to an event that has already occurred. This is the situation at the Prado museum (see entry case study 12.1). The chairman, Mr Serra, is seeking to make the Prado react to its current situation, which has been some time in the making, by seeking to tackle inadequate budgets, lack of devolved financial control and a leaking roof. In contrast, proactive change is where an organisation plans and prepares for expected and anticipated events and maybe even how to deal with unexpected events.

Unexpected events include shock occurrences, such as a chemical company experiencing a leak or explosion, or a food manufacturer suffering contamination of food or drink products with glass or poison. These types of events are rare and unpredictable, but organisations can plan for the steps they will take in such circumstances. The planning should cover what action should be taken and who in the organisation is responsible for taking it. The issues that should be covered include dealing with the event as soon as it happens, for example recalling all food or drink products that might be affected and offering a full refund, which is important if the dent to consumer confidence is to be minimised; liaising with the emergency services and investigating authorities, important in the example of the chemical company leak or explosion; dealing with those members of the public affected; and liaising with the media, the effectiveness of which is likely to affect public perception of the organisation and consumer confidence.

Major organisational changes in size and structure will affect hierarchical and reporting relationships, along with communication and decision-making systems. An organisation that decreases the number of middle managers it employs will also be reducing its size and that of its hierarchy. Hence the structure of the organisation will be flatter, and more communication will need to occur between those at the top and those further down. At the same time, decision making will have to be either decentralised to those further down the organisation or centralised with those at the top.

A change in organisational culture, which is difficult to achieve, is likely to involve changes in personalities and the position these people occupy in the organisation. This was demonstrated in the case of the Prado museum with the arrival of the new chairman Mr Serra, the departure of the director Mr Checa and the arrival of his successor Mr Zugaza. This means that leadership styles and the way in which people are motivated will change. Different organisational cultural styles are examined in Chapters 1 and 2. For employees of an organisation undergoing change, the changes will be felt in the tasks and activities they perform on a daily basis as part of their jobs. This may include changes in the way the job is carried out. The content of a particular job may change completely or only slightly. This will occur at the Prado museum if Mr Serra and Mr Zugaza succeed in driving through change, as the day-to-day activities will change to take account of the introduction of new staff on flexible employment contracts, better pay and performance reviews. Technology may alter the way someone's job is done and the way work is co-ordinated in the organisation, the obvious example being the introduction of audio guides at the Prado museum.

✓ Check your understanding

Do you understand the different types of change an organisation can experience?

Check your understanding by listing possible types of change an organisation may experience.

The process of change

In this section an overall view is taken of the process of change and the issues affecting the managers and stakeholders involved.

Lewin[1] suggests that change is the outcome of the impact of driving forces on restraining forces, more commonly known as force field analysis – *see* Figure 12.2. This can be thought of as the status quo that is under pressure to change. The resulting change is a direct outcome of either the driving forces or the restraining forces being more powerful. It is normal for the driving forces of change to have economic attributes. These economic attributes may arise from the external environment as a result of macroeconomic changes or because of internal issues, e.g. the need to cut costs and improve profit margins. One example of this is the shoe manufacturer and retailer Clarks reorganising and restructuring its US operations, when in the financial year ending 31 January 1996 trading profit was only £700 000, compared with £3.6 million in the previous year.

In most organisations undergoing change, at least part of the workforce will be dedicated and faithful to the existing work practices, as in the case of the Prado museum's life-long tenured civil service staff, who see no reason for

Figure 12.2
Lewin's force field analysis

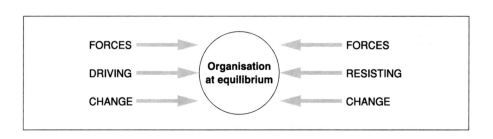

change. The news that these practices will have to change will leave staff feeling concerned about their jobs and future with the organisation. Their reluctance to accept and adopt suggested changes forms the restraining forces that contribute to the unbalancing of the status quo. The restraining forces will seek to persuade the organisation to discontinue or alter the recommended changes and counteract the driving forces of change.

Managers in organisations experiencing change obviously need to be aware of both driving and restraining forces. The managers involved should seek to communicate strong justification of the changes by offering a clear and unclouded explanation of the reasons for the changes and any advances in employee empowerment that will result. This was clearly so when Clarks reorganised and restructured its US operations, resulting in a change in the way shoes were produced for and sold to the US market. American staff were given the freedom to redesign and adapt UK designs for the US market. This resulted in selling US-designed shoes to American customers, instead of thrusting UK-designed shoes at them.

However, in planning such significant change a careful balance needs to be struck between providing too much information, which may raise fears and queries that cannot yet be dealt with, and providing inadequate information, which leaves people feeling that they have been told nothing and are being kept in the dark. Hence change requires strong and effective leadership from the managers involved, particularly if structural and cultural changes are to occur. The leadership in any new working teams or groups will have to be particularly strong and focused if the implemented change is to be successful.

A strong and effective change manager will disperse resistance to change by highlighting early achievements resulting from the change, which will also help maintain the momentum of the change programme and prevent it suffering from setbacks and periods of slow progress. Recognition that not everyone will support the change and that the feelings of those who are likely to be hurt by it require sensitive handling will help the change process to be managed successfully.

 Check your understanding

Do you understand what is meant by 'force field analysis'?

Check your understanding by explaining what a force field analysis demonstrates.

The change process model

The Lewin model[2] was developed to identify and examine the three stages of the change process. The first stage is unfreezing current attitudes and behaviour – *see* Figure 12.3. This unfreezing stage takes the view that if attitudes and behaviour are to change, then old behaviour must come to be regarded

Figure 12.3

The change process model

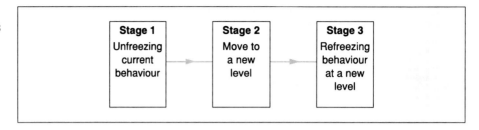

Stage 1
Unfreezing current behaviour

Stage 2
Move to a new level

Stage 3
Refreezing behaviour at a new level

as unsuitable and must stop. Hence the requirement for change must be appreciated directly by the people to be affected by the change, as it cannot be imposed on them if the change process is to succeed. If Mr Serra and Mr Zugaza are to succeed at the Prado museum, they need to convince the civil service staff of the need for change, an extremely difficult task as they have rejected the 'carrot of better pay' (see entry case study 12.1). The unfreezing process may be achieved by realisation among the people involved that change is required for some reason. Common driving forces of change often result from commercial pressures, which include the need for increased sales or market share, better profitability or more efficient production. The unfreezing process requires employees affected by the change to understand and be clearly informed of the difficulties confronting the organisation. This involves information on the current problems being communicated to all employees. The current problems may include issues such as reducing market share, poor quality of product or service, or inefficient production levels when compared with competition. The civil servants at the Prado museum will need to understand the problems of the poor physical state of the building and its extention, the poor financial state of affairs, the demand for better services in terms of guidance and information which visitors expect, which will in return require more staff to be employed by the museum.

The second stage of Lewin's change process model is moving to a new level. A search for answers to the difficulties faced by the organisation has to occur. This involves reviewing alternative solutions, the examination of changing values and culture within the organisation, and an assessment of the organisational structure that would most suit the changing organisation. The people affected by the change should continue to receive regular updating communications about possible answers and solutions to the difficulties faced by the organisation. These informing and updating communications should be both verbal, via meetings, and written, for example via a newsletter. The use of meetings allows people's ideas and views on the proposed changes to be gathered and their questions, queries and fears to be addressed. Issuing a newsletter allows what has been discussed at meetings to be confirmed and is also a useful summary, particularly for anyone who was not able to be there. Meetings should be organised and structured so that all those affected by the change have the opportunity to be involved in the debate and discussions. If the change is significant and large numbers of people are involved, a series of meetings covering different departments, sections or divisions will be required throughout the period in which the change occurs.

Solutions and answers to the difficulties faced by the organisation need to be developed and the essential changes planned. Hence there is a need to continue communicating with those affected by the change. Once this has been achieved, the implementation of the planned changes can be arranged. Then the chosen solutions can start to be implemented, which may necessitate running in parallel new and current systems and methods of working. This allows the newly implemented solutions to be assessed as working satisfactorily, before the old method or system of working is withdrawn. There should then be a final review and tweaking of systems and methods of working to ensure that the required level of work and satisfaction is being achieved by the people involved.

The third stage of Lewin's change process model is refreezing attitudes and behaviour at the new level. This takes place once acceptable solutions have been found. The refreezing stage involves positive reinforcement and support for the implemented changes. This can be done by highlighting improvements in difficult areas that have occurred as a result of the changes, for example an upturn in sales or improvement in quality, which could include testimony from a satisfied customer reproduced in a company newsletter. People from other parts of the organisation not directly affected by the changes also need to be informed of what has been altered.

☑ Check your understanding

Do you understand Lewin's change process model?

Check your understanding by naming the three stages of Lewin's change process model and summarise what happens in organisations experiencing each of the three stages.

An alternative view of the change process is presented by Burnes.[3] He suggests that the change process consists of three interlinked elements: objectives and outcomes, planning the change, and people – *see* Figure 12.4.

Figure 12.4
The change process by Burnes

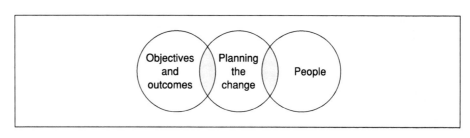

Objectives and outcomes

In assessing the objectives and outcomes, Burnes presents four phases that organisations should work through in deciding whether change is appropriate. First, a trigger for organisational change should exist and fall into one of the following broad categories: the requirement for change is core to organisational strategy; better performance is a core theme of competitive strategy; serious problems exist with current performance; or opportunities exist that will provide the organisation with a greater return than that currently achieved.

Once organisational change has been triggered, the second phase, the remit, is entered. Drawing up the remit is about establishing clear agreement concerning where the accountability and authority to instigate change exist in the organisation. This needs to be undertaken prior to proceeding further with the change process. The accountability and authority to instigate the change process rest with senior management in a bureaucratic and hierarchical organisation, but will be devolved in an organisation with a flatter structure and more modern approach to management. The remit also needs to outline the objectives of the change programme along with the time in which the change can be expected to be implemented and achieve its objectives and outcomes. Finally, it is very necessary for any remit concerning change to make crystal clear that a full range of options, not just one or two, needs to be examined and evaluated in deciding what change should take place.

Once the remit is established, an assessment team should be confirmed to explain the difficulty or opportunity facing the organisation, explore possible options, discuss the problems/opportunities and options with interested parties, and make recommendations about the way forward. The assessment team will usually contain representation from a wide range of people, for example those affected by the change, specialist staff (such as finance, personnel), senior management and in some cases a change agent – an outside consultant or facilitator who promotes and stimulates the change process.

The assessment team will seek to explain the difficulty or opportunity facing the organisation by gathering information and speaking to those directly and indirectly involved. This is followed by establishing possible options for dealing with the difficulty or opportunity. The options or solutions that offer the greatest benefit and are practical should be identified. The difficulties and possible solutions need to be discussed with the stakeholders affected by the change process. Finally, the assessment team should present its recommendations to those responsible for making the final decision on what change will occur. Those responsible may be senior management and/or those affected by the change, and they will decide to accept, reject or modify the proposals.

Planning the change

Once the remit for change and an assessment of the change required have been settled, the planning of the actual change which needs to occur and its implementation can be undertaken. The initial stage is to confirm the change management team, which will usually include many of the people who were members of the assessment team. Clarity, in terms of where and to whom the change management team reports, along with how it gains access to resources, is paramount, as during a period of change ambiguity can arise very easily.

The function of the change management team is to devise a schedule for change, specifying the tasks and activities that need to occur if successful change is to result. The tasks and activities should link directly to the object-ives and outcomes of the change and be expressed in very focused terms if they are to be carried out accurately and within the desired timescale. This requires the support of those in favour of the change to be harnessed and used to progress the change programme. In a programme of major change it is important to review events periodically and assess whether the tasks and activities have been carried out correctly and are in fact achieving the objectives and outcomes of the change. In addition, such reviews are likely to yield lessons for future change programmes. Finally, most programmes of major change will require some form of training to allow those affected by the change to cope and perform well under the new working conditions. The training required can take many forms and may, for example, include skills development to cope with a new quality programme or technical training to allow staff to operate new equipment, machinery and computers.

People

The third and final element of Burnes's change process model is people. Whatever the change undertaken, people are normally part of the change process and therefore have to be given consideration. Burnes proposes that in implementing change there are three people-related issues that must be handled if the change is to succeed and the organisation flourish: people must be responsive to the need for change, they should be involved in the change process, and the impetus resulting from the change should be sustained.

Ensuring that people are responsive to organisational change is difficult, as it involves moving from the familiar to the unfamiliar. Therefore organisa-tions need to ensure that the sources of resistance to change and how to deal with them are understood. This is exactly what Mr Serra and Mr Zugaza at the Prado museum are seeking to do (see entry case study 12.1). This can be done by making sure that employees are familiar with company plans and the pressures faced by the organisation from, for example, customers, com-petitors and suppliers. In this context, the focus of the information provided to employees should be to show that change is undertaken to secure, not jeopardise, the future of the organisation. Accordingly, the difference between current and desired future performance should be outlined in a manner that allows employees to relate the proposed change to themselves and their individual/group/section performance. This allows employees to think about how such improvement may be made and to contribute their own ideas to the change process. The successful achievement of change to meet the intended objectives and outcomes can be publicised to promote further change or change in a different part of the organisation, as required. In doing this mistakes do not have to be swept under the carpet, but should be regarded as a learning process for future change projects.

The management of a changing organisation also has to be responsive to change and understand the anxieties and apprehension felt by those affected directly by the changes. Significant concern about change in an organisation may indicate that all is not right with the proposed alterations, and further consideration of the suggested changes may be needed. The resistance to change that arises from anxiety and apprehension may be at least partly over-come by involving the people affected in the change process. Most change programmes are long and complex and if people are to be properly involved, they have to be so from beginning to end, in the development, planning and implementation of the changes.

Involvement should start with clear and regular communication with those affected. The communication process will involve the assessment team and the change management team and should seek to explain the context of the proposed change, its details and its consequences. The communication process should be two way. The people affected by the changes need to listen and take on board what is planned, and it is equally necessary for the change management team to listen to those affected and their views and ideas about what it is appropriate to change. This may result in the change management team reviewing their ideas and assumptions about what change is necessary. They should gain assistance in the change process rather than resistance to it. This can be encouraged by making every effort to involve those most closely affected and giving them responsibility for the change project.

Once the change has been developed, planned and implemented, the challenge for the organisation is to sustain its impetus. This is important, as if the impetus created by change is not sustained, there exists a danger that people will revert to old behaviour and past ways of doing things. In order to sustain the impetus, the organisation should consider several issues, starting with the provision of additional resources, both financial and human. These would provide clear support for staff striving to uphold previous levels of output for the duration of the turbulent period of change. The change man-agement team should also be given support and not be ignored, as they have been charged with motivating others and dealing with problems associated with the change process. If support for the change management team is not forthcoming, its members are likely to become disheartened and demotivated and will no longer be in a position to support and motivate others.

The development of new skills and knowledge among staff and leadership styles among managers is frequently required as part of the process of change. Backing for the process can also be provided by the organisation meeting the challenge of allowing staff and management to gain the required knowledge, skills and leadership style in a non-threatening and encouraging manner.

Sustaining the impetus of change can be reinforced by rewarding behaviour that supports the change and the new way of doing things. The rewards can be monetary or simply praise for achieving success in the changed organisation.

The process of change is an intricate blend of setting objectives, planning the change and managing the people involved, with all three areas involving gathering information and making decisions about what is most important. However, in many instances change will continue to occur long after the actual programme for change has been successfully implemented. This can become a pattern of continuous improvement and change.

✓ Check your understanding

Do you understand the Burnes view of organisational change?

Check your understanding by naming and explaining the areas in the Burnes model for organisational change.

Changing organisational structure

Structure and culture are the two most significant things that an organisation can change about itself. This section will look at changing structure and the next section at changing culture. The five basic organisational structures are identified and discussed in Chapter 1. Thompson[4] identifies four determinants of organisational structure: size, tasks, environment and ideology – *see* Figure 12.5.

Size

The size of an organisation will influence which structure is most suitable. The most suitable structure is that which allows the best and most effective communication and co-ordination within the organisation. A large organisation or one that has grown in size in terms of more and bigger markets, a greater range of products and services, an increasing number of employees or a greater number of factories or outlets will require a different structure from a small business that has just opened its first factory or outlet. The centralised

Figure 12.5
Determinants of organisational structure

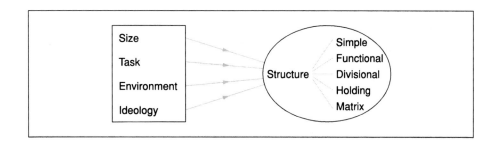

simple and functional structures are suitable for smaller organisations and offer a number of advantages and disadvantages, but these cease to be appropriate once an organisation has expanded significantly – *see* Chapter 1.

The question of structure can be illustrated by ICI and the dilemma the company faced in March 1998. It had just sold off its bulk chemicals businesses, retaining its paints business with the ICI Dulux brand, and had acquired other branded products such as Polyfilla. The debate centred around whether to keep the paints business together with the other branded goods or to separate it. ICI's view was that there were considerable benefits in keeping its paints business and the ICI Dulux brand together with its other branded products. However, one of its main rivals, Kalon, which specialised in paints, gained a much better profit margin than ICI from paint. The alternative view was that paint is a bulk chemicals business and there is no benefit in keeping it with branded goods, so it should be spun off into its own separate division. This was the approach of another of ICI's rivals in the paint business, Courtaulds, which had done just that. If ICI kept paints and branded chemicals together and the business did well, shareholders would be delighted; but if profits were not good and shares performed poorly, shareholders were likely to question the structure of the company.[5]

Tasks

A large and complex organisation with both interlinked and dissimilar tasks and activities will have a crucial need for effective co-ordination and communication. Where an organisation's tasks and activities are complex and interlinked, the most suitable structure will be decentralised such as the divisional or matrix structure. In contrast, if all the tasks and activities carried out by the organisation are dissimilar and unconnected, the holding company structure may be appropriate – *see* Chapter 1.

Environment

The external environment of an organisation exerts pressure on it to change. These external environmental pressures result from all areas of the external environment, typically including political, economic, sociocultural and technological pressures (*see* Chapters 8 and 9). Other external environmental pressures arise from changing customer demands and market size, as well as the behaviour of competing organisations (*see* Chapters 4 and 10). The key issue for organisations to consider is their ability to prioritise and select which pressures to respond to and the degree and speed of response required.

An organisation with a centralised structure will be much less flexible and therefore less able to respond rapidly to major change. In contrast, an organisation with a decentralised structure will be able to react more quickly to major change if required to do so, but the disadvantage is the greater difficulty in co-ordinating an organisation-wide response to change.

Ideology

The logical argument here is that the longer an organisation has operated with a particular structure, the more difficult it will be to change it. The difficulties will arise as people who are very familiar with their specific jobs and responsibilities are likely to be set in their ways and wary of change. This will have to be overcome, as described in the section on the process of change earlier in this chapter. A structure that allows the complexity, similarities and dissimilarities in the organisation's tasks and activities to be managed so that it operates both efficiently and effectively should be aimed for. This may mean that a new structure has to be designed that uses the best ideas from the five basic organisational structures.

☑ Check your understanding

Do you understand the determinants of structure?

Check your understanding by explaining how each determinant of structure may shape the structure of an organisation.

Greiner's model

The changes that an organisation's structure may undergo are summarised in Greiner's model – *see* Figure 12.6. This relates growth rate, age and size of the organisation to five phases of growth and development.[6] Each phase of growth consists of an evolutionary stage and a revolutionary stage. Hence it should be clearly understood that 'each phase is both an effect of the previous phase and a cause for the next phase'.[7] An evolutionary stage is one in which there is a dominant management style that is successful. In a revolutionary stage there is a dominant management problem that has to be resolved for the organisation to continue to grow and move on to the next evolutionary stage. The rate of growth is indicated by the steepness of the line on Greiner's model, a steep line indicating high growth and a gradual line indicating slow growth.

The key impact of an organisation's age is that the older an organisation, the more likely attitudes and behaviour are to be engrained, resulting in a potentially greater resistance to change. The larger the organisation, the more extensive the task of ensuring that communication, co-ordination and interdependence of the organisation's activities are achieved. An increase in both age and size of an organisation usually suggests that it has grown steadily over a number of years, which is termed a stage of evolution. During the stages of evolution (*see* Figure 12.6) the style of management behaviour continues to be more or less stable, with only minor adjustments required to ensure that the organisation is able to perform its tasks and activities effectively. In contrast,

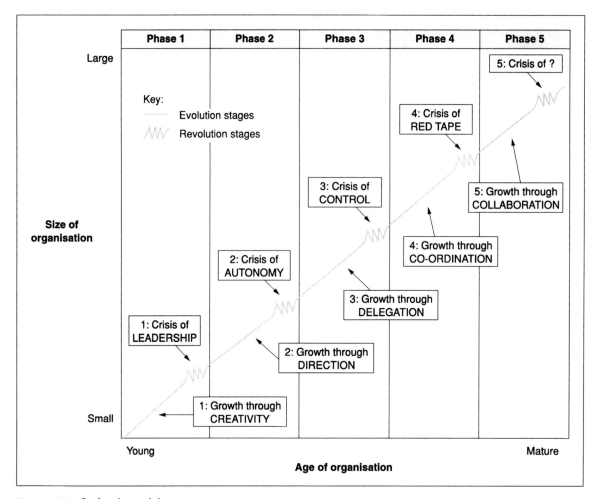

Figure 12.6 **Greiner's model**

periods of great flux and upheaval in an organisation's life are referred to as stages of revolution.

A stage of revolution is when old management and work practices are put under pressure from new requirements brought about by the increasing age and size of the organisation. The stages of revolution are shown on Greiner's model as crises with which the organisation has to cope if it is to pass successfully into the next stage of relative stability or evolution.

In the summer of 1999, the UK Passport Agency was in the midst of a period of revolution, with the installation of a new computer system and change in the law requiring all children under 16 who were not currently on a parent's passport to have their own passport. This created a crisis for the Passport Agency, as the number of applications for passports rose and waiting times for the issue of new passports also increased, from 6–8 weeks to as much as 15 weeks in some cases. This resulted in people panicking and believing that they were not going to receive their new passport in time to go on their summer holiday.

If an organisation is unable to deal successfully with a stage of revolution, it may be that it stagnates and eventually goes into decline, losing customers and market share, selling out-of-date products and services and having to make people redundant. The Passport Agency is the only issuer of British passports in the UK, therefore the government was anxious to ensure that the system worked. The crisis of the summer of 1999 was dealt with by the introduction of emergency measures enabling post offices to extend the expiry date of existing passports by two years.

Phase 1 – Growth through creativity and the crisis of leadership

In phase one of Greiner's model, an organisation's energies are directed towards developing and selling the product or service. Hence minimal energy goes into management activities and communication is regular and informal. The management of such an organisation reacts to feedback from customers and the marketplace. This type of organisation will typically adopt a simple structure (*see* Chapter 1). As the size and age of the organisation increase, a crisis of leadership will occur. The organisation's leader will be under considerable stress and unable to manage a growing organisation on their own via informal communication and co-ordination. There will be a clear need for greater management expertise in the organisation if the workforce and resources are to be handled effectively.

Phase 2 – Growth through direction and crisis of autonomy

The crisis of leadership is resolved through 'professionalising' the organisation. This involves any number of the following occurring: specialised managers being introduced to the organisation; restructuring, typically the functional structure being adopted; implementation of formal control and communication systems; and the development of a decision-making hierarchy. Professionalising of the organisation helps iron out the difficulties arising from running a growing organisation very informally and allows the organisation to continue to grow in age and size. After this further stage of evolution, 'growth through direction', another crisis occurs, this time the crisis of autonomy. The lack of autonomy results in employees feeling restricted by centralisation and the formal control systems that have been implemented. There is also a lack of opportunity for employees to act on their own initiative.

Phase 3 – Growth through delegation and crisis of control

The crisis of autonomy is handled by a move towards decentralisation, which gives more responsibility to plant and sales managers and provides an opportunity for employees to act on their own initiative. This is supported by implementing a structure such as the divisional structure, which uses profit centres and profit-sharing schemes or bonuses to motivate managers to perform well. Short- and medium-term planning is left to middle management and their workforce, while senior managers deal with long-term or strategic planning. The crisis in this phase is one of control. The move to decentralisation results in management feeling a loss of control over an organisation with a complex and diverse range of products and services in different and unrelated industries.

**Phase 4 –
Growth through
co-ordination and
crisis of red tape**

The crisis of control is tackled by the introduction of more formal planning procedures and an increase of staff in roles concerned with company-wide control and management of the workforce and resources. Critical functions in the organisation will be centralised, while decentralised units that show some relation or similarity will be merged into product groups. This should allow managers in the organisation to take a corporate-wide perspective rather than merely a local view of their own department or division.

The crisis arising from greater co-ordination is one of red tape. This is indicated by a lack of confidence in the relationship between staff in the organisation and headquarters, from where many of the co-ordination systems will have originated. The co-ordination systems may no longer support the local market conditions in which employees have to operate. In summary, there is an expansion of systems that is too extensive and rigid to allow an organisation still increasing in size and age to operate effectively. Innovation, which can aid organisational growth, will also be inhibited.

**Phase 5 –
Growth through
collaboration and
the ? crisis**

The red tape crisis is overcome by an increase in team and cross-functional activity, which usually involves the organisation restructuring to a matrix structure. The greater flexibility of the matrix structure allows team working and cross-functional activity to occur naturally. The strong co-ordinating management of the previous phase is replaced by social control and self-discipline of both individual workers and the teams in which they operate.

Greiner anticipates that Phase 5 may be concluded by a crisis of 'psychological saturation', where employees are exhausted by the demands of teamwork and the need for innovation. In conclusion, he suggests that organisations will adopt a dual structure. First, there will be a 'habit' structure within which employees carry out their routine, day-to-day work. Second, there will be a 'reflective' structure for 'stimulating perspectives and personal enrichment'.[8] This will be a structure that allows employees to refuel and may include things such as flexible working hours, revolving jobs and sabbaticals.

In conclusion, managers should be able to recognise the phase of Greiner's model at which their organisation starts currently and its associated organisational structure and features, and hence be able to identify the next phase of growth. This should encourage the development of the key skills and strengths required to get the organisation through the next crisis or stage of revolution and to continue success in the next stage of evolution. Moreover, progression from one phase to the next is not automatic and managers must consciously act to move the organisation through the rough revolutionary stage to the next higher evolutionary stage.

✓ Check your understanding

Do you understand the five phases of Greiner's model?

Check your understanding by naming and briefly describing the phases of Greiner's model.

Making cultural change successful

Deal and Kennedy[9] outline seven elements required for successful cultural change to be achieved.

Position a hero in charge of the process

Deal and Kennedy define a hero as a high achiever in the organisation and someone who personifies the organisation's cultural values and hence pro-avides an explicit role model for employees. Heroes 'show every employee "here's what you have to do to succeed around here."'[10] A hero put in charge of the change process will have to believe strongly in and be committed to the proposed changes. The person or hero in charge of the change process needs to inspire belief in and commitment to the change among the affected workforce.

Recognise a real threat from outside

Major cultural change in organisations requires sound reasoning before the change process can be initiated, as well as the appointment of a hero. An organisation's external environment may alter to such an extent that the culture of the organisation and the external environment no longer match one another. The more significant the threat posed to the organisation by the mismatch between its external environment and culture, the more likely it is that the culture can be successfully changed.

Make transition rituals the pivotal elements of change

The involvement of the people to be affected by change in the change pro-cess is a common recommendation of both academics and practitioners. Deal and Kennedy suggest a 'transitional ritual' or stage. This is where old ways of doing and organising things cease and new working relationships are established. This is a period of change in which people are encouraged to adopt new work patterns without rushing, while at the same time resisting the temptation to return to the old ways of working. Eventually the new working patterns and relationships become established as the norm.

Provide transition training in new values and behaviour patterns

New working practices and relationships need help to become established. Hence a programme of change will have to be available to all the employees affected. A culture change programme should focus on new values, new behaviour and new language if new working practices and new relationships are to become permanent and last in the long term.

Bringing in outside shamans

An organisation experiencing cultural change needs to drive the change from inside, hence the need for good management and clear direction. However, an outside 'shaman' or consultant can be useful in helping the people affected by the change span the gap between the two different organisational cultures. This can be done by defusing the friction and strife and helping those affected by the change see that the way forward suggested by the change in culture can work successfully.

Build tangible symbols of the new direction

People in an organisation affected by cultural change need to see and feel the effects of the change if they are to consider moving forward with the organisation and its cultural change. A good example of this would be a well-managed alteration to the structure of the organisation, as this would send a clear and tangible message concerning the direction in which the organisation was now heading.

Insist on the importance of security in transition

Proposed change in an organisation will always create uncertainty and as such needs to be minimised. The greatest uncertainty that people will feel is that surrounding the security of their jobs, and this needs to be made clear and dealt with swiftly. Those people who are staying with the organisation need to be informed that this is the case. Equally, those who are to be bought off or made redundant also need to be told. Dealing with the issue of job security in an unambiguous way is an crucial part of effective change.

Change is sometimes required in an organisation. Its result can be good or bad. The certainty of change is that it is usually risky, expensive and time consuming. However, if the managers involved are sensitive to the organisational culture, the change process can be managed successfully.

✓ Check your understanding

Do you understand Deal and Kennedy's seven elements for successful cultural change?

Check your understanding by briefly describing the seven elements for successful cultural change.

Summary

This chapter gave an overview of organisational change in its earlier sections. It then went on to examine two entities that are explored in earlier chapters and are also often changed by organisations, namely structure (Chapter 1) and culture (Chapter 2). The following summary covers all aspects of this chapter.

1. The causes of organisational change can arise from the external environment faced by a company, i.e. the PEST factors, competitors, markets and customers. Equally causes of change can arise from inside an organisation, namely the employees, trade unions, and individual departments or divisions.

2. The changes organisations experience may include alterations to size, structure and culture. Changes of this nature often result in changes to leadership, hierarchy and the decision-making process. Also the tasks and activities carried out by staff on a day-to-day basis may change.

3   The process of change is summed up by Lewin as being the outcome of the impact of driving forces upon restraining forces, which is commonly referred to as force field analysis. Certain stakeholders, e.g. employees, may be concerned about their future with the organisation and seek to resist change, while managers concerned about the long-term survival of the business seek to drive change.

4   Lewin also developed the change process model, which identifies three stages of the change process. First is the unfreezing stage, in which current behaviour has to become viewed as unsuitable. The second stage is moving to a new level, which involves finding and establishing new behaviours. The third stage is refreezing, when new behaviours become established and the accepted norm.

5   The Burnes model for organisational change identifies three areas which need to be tackled. The first, objectives and outcomes, involves identifying the trigger for organisational change, followed by agreement as to exactly who is responsible for instigating the change. Next an assessment team should be appointed to identify and recommend the changes which need to occur.

6   The second area in the Burnes model is planning the change, which initially includes confirming the change management team, who it reports to and the resources to which it has access. The function of the team is to devise a plan for undertaking and implementing change, which should link directly to the recommendations presented by the assessment team in the first stage, 'objectives and outcomes'.

7   The third area of the Burnes organisational change model is people. Implementing change needs to ensure people are responsive to change, involved in the change process and can sustain the change once it is implemented.

8   There are four determinants of organisational structure: size, task, environment and ideology. Changes to any of these for an organisation can be a driver for change in organisational structure.

9   Greiner's model is useful in looking at the different structures an organisation may adopt. Greiner argues that each phase or structure ultimately sows the seeds of its own decline and the move to a new structure needs to be actively managed for the period of revolution to be got through.

10 Deal and Kennedy identify seven elements required for successful cultural change. These are 'position a hero in charge of the process', 'recognise a real threat from outside', 'make transition rituals the pivotal elements of change', 'provide transition training in new values and behaviour patterns', 'bring in outside shamans', 'build tangible symbols of the new direction', and 'insist on the importance of security in transition'.